Light Broke

into

My Darkness

Dan Miller

ISBN 979-8-89428-644-0 (paperback)
ISBN 979-8-89428-645-7 (digital)

Christian Faith Publishing
832 Park Avenue
Meadville, PA 16335
www.christianfaithpublishing.com

Printed in the United States of America

I was once a young man, empty and void of purpose in life. I was engulfed in the pain, suffering, and death in the world. In that reality, I did not see a possible future or hope for myself. I begin to say, "There has to be more to life than this." I had no idea at the time, but that little confession would set me on a course to pursue the meaning of life. As a kid, I was no stranger to church and had prayed that God would forgive me for all my sins per instruction. I was presented with a God who was distant and angry with me. All I knew of his character was that He was going to judge me for all my wrongdoings and send me to hell. I was not, however, told that he loved me and wanted to have a relationship with me.

As time went by, I lost interest in church and began to attend less often. Because if God is distant and angry, why would I want to be with Him? Most of my formative years were without a father in my life. My earthly father was distant. He would come and go throughout the years and would be with us for a little while, then he would be gone. Whenever he was around, he never showed interest in my well-being and balanced this with explosive anger. When my mom became frustrated at me, she would turn me over to him for "punishment." He never comforted me. He never told me he loved me. This was what I thought a father was. As a result, when the church world presented God to me as angry and judgmental, I wanted no part of it and ran. I was a lost soul for the first twenty years of my life. I moved out of my mom's house and into an apartment with a friend of mine. We worked our jobs, and then on the weekends we would go out drinking and spend all our money. I experimented with drugs such as marijuana and alcohol but never really wanted them. I only used them to mask the emptiness I was experiencing, but things started to change.

Unknowingly, God began to stir my heart. I remember starting to ask questions. One Saturday night, when my friends and I came home, everybody was smoking marijuana, and I just had this thought: "Guys, think about this. We go out every weekend, we spend our money, we come back, and we do it all over again the next week. Do you guys see a cycle here? There must be more to life than this." At that point, I didn't realize that God had begun to draw me and reveal to me the darkness of my situation.

One Saturday night, all my friends had gotten together early and drank beer and smoked a little marijuana. We all took some drugs, loaded up in the car together, and started heading to the club. Joining us that night was another friend from my old high school. He wanted to try some of the drugs we were taking. I told him he didn't need this stuff. (Do you see the change of perspective as a result of God drawing me?) I knew he went to church, and I didn't want him to go down the wrong path that I was on.

That's when it all began. As we were pulling into the parking lot of the nightclub, I suddenly heard a voice speak to me as if out of nowhere and said, *"Danny, you don't need this stuff either!"* I asked out loud, "Who said that?" No one said anything. It was so strange, I just shrugged it off for the moment. We went into the nightclub; the music was so loud, and we could barely hear one another. Walking into the club, we noticed it was a packed house that night, and out of the crowd, this guy began to come toward me. It was unusual that I even noticed him coming toward me because of the drugs, but his eye contact froze me in place. As he got closer to me, I watched him intently, trying not to make it obvious that I was aware of his approach. He seemed suspect to me. He had long hair, a biker jacket, biker boots, and a biker wallet sticking out of his back pocket. He walked right up to me, so I braced myself for anything. He looked at me and said, "Do you know Jesus?" I responded to make sure I heard him correctly, "Do I know Jesus?" He said, "Yes." I thought about that for a moment, and I repeated the question to myself, "Do I know Jesus?" That question completely took me off guard, as it was definitely not what I was expecting. I sat there contemplating it for a moment, and I heard another voice. I began to realize that this voice was familiar and had appeared to me before over the years. This was the first time I recognized the voice of Satan…he whispered to me, *"Tell him you know him; tell him you know him!"* Rather emphatically. So yes. I lied to the man. I said I knew him. He was kind of taken aback by that. The music was still blaring through the sound system, and people were pressing in all around. Although it didn't seem to matter at the moment. The guy just kept looking at me. So finally, I said, "Yeah, man, what is it now?" He had this big grin on his face, and he exclaimed, "It's great, isn't it?" I said, "Yeah, man," thinking to myself. Please. Won't this guy go away? Finally, he turned and left, and as he walked off, I heard that voice again that I heard in the car (not Satan this time). He said to me, *"No, Danny, you don't know me!"* At this point, I yelled out with concern and confusion, "Who is talking to me?!" My friends were like, "Man, are you okay?" I said, "Yes. Someone is talking to me, man." They said, tapping me on the shoulder, "Man, it's just the drugs. Calm down, you'll be okay." I backed into the wall and wondered, "Man, what drugs did I take?"

As we were leaving that night, we ran into some college kids passing out fliers outside the club. The fliers were for this rock crusade or something like that. So we talked for a while, and they invited us to come to a free concert they were having. After asking them where this concert was, they said it was being held in a church. I said, "You are having a rock concert in your church?"

They said, "Kind of."

I said, "Kind of? What does that mean?"

"Well, it's free, and we're going to have a speaker who used to be in a rock 'n' roll band."

I thought, *Well, that's cool.* Maybe we could check that out. So after the small talk, they asked if they could pray for us. I said *sure.* So we got into this big circle—all my friends and their friends and they all wanted to hold hands. That was kind of strange to me, but we did, and one guy on the other side of the circle began to pray. As he was praying, this overwhelming presence of peace came over me. It seemed to go right through my body. All the effects of the alcohol and the drugs just left me, and I was completely sober. I looked up and said, "Man, what just happened?"

One of them responded, "What do you mean?"

"I felt this peace go through me, and I'm completely sober."

He said, "Man, that's the presence of God. God has touched you tonight!"

I said, "Wow. I've never felt anything like that before in my life!"

Well, the next day came. I had to go help a girlfriend of mine move some furniture for her brother. It was a beautiful day, with temperatures in the midseventies. Though this is pleasant lounging weather, I overheated because of the exertion of moving furniture and the alcohol dehydration from the previous night. So I decided to take a break and walk outside. I saw a trampoline out in the backyard and lay down on it to cool off. As

I was lying there, I felt this peace go through my body again! It was that overwhelming peace that I felt the night before, but it began to leave. I said, "Wait, please don't leave…" Then I had this thought go through my mind, *Remember you said you were going to the rock crusade tonight?* I said, "Oh yeah, I did say that. Man, I need to go." At that moment, my girlfriend walked outside, and I said I had to get back. She asked why, and I told her that my friends and I had plans to go to church. She said, "Going to church?" I know what a shocker. She had never heard me say anything like that before. And neither have I up to this point. But for some reason, I knew I needed to go. She dropped me off after a fight and a quick breakup, and my friends were waiting. "Hey, man, are we going tonight?" I said, "Yeah, we're going." So we got ready and hopped in my little Mazda RX7, a two-seater with a hatchback. I managed to get two of us in the front and two in the back. And off we went. As we were traveling I-59/20 through downtown Birmingham, two cars went flying past me on both sides. It appears they were road-raging. The car on my right side jumped in front of my car and decided he was going to ram the car on his left. He jammed his car into the guardrail, and I hit the brakes. I thought we were going to wreck. (Bear with me, this was epic.) I was able to gear down, cut the wheel, and get around them. I said, "Man, that was close. Scary too." I knew I was supposed to keep driving for some reason, so even after that, we pressed on. We finally got to this church, and we all walked in together. I felt out of place, understandably. My friends and I didn't necessarily dress like church people. We dressed like bar people. If there is such a thing, we just didn't fit in. So we found a seat and sat down. This band walked up on stage and began to play some rock music. But it was unlike any rock music I'd ever heard. The lyrics in this music seemed to be about God. I had never heard anything like that before, and I was amazed that there was even music like this. After they had finished, this man walked out on stage. He started sharing about his life as a rock 'n' roll musician and told story after story of how that industry drove him into a life of darkness. He would tell stories of how the music itself was causing teens to commit suicide at alarming rates. How the music played backward had subliminal messages that would tell kids to commit suicide. That scared me something fierce, and when he played one of those albums, I was familiar with it backward. I thought to myself, *That's crazy.* He went ahead to say how empty he had become inside by living in that lifestyle for so long. It had driven him into depression and deep darkness. He said he'd begin to search for the meaning of life (see a recurring theme?). It was then and there that I realized I wasn't the only one looking for answers. As he continued, he revealed how, at the end of it all, he was broken, lonely, depressed, afraid, and lost. He had no hope and a lot of regret. I said to myself, "He is reading my mail now for sure." At his lowest point and on the verge of suicide, someone shared Jesus with him. He heard the message of God's grace—how God loved him and had a better plan for his life than he did. God then took his broken life and turned him into another man. How God had forgiven all his sins and washed them away as if they never existed. Jesus took all his sin and shame upon himself on the cross and died. He said he gave his life to Jesus and how Jesus gave him a new life. He removed all his guilt and condemnation and then set him on a course to experience peace, joy, and life everlasting. He said, "God took a nobody and made a somebody out of me." God called him to be an evangelist and to share with others about Jesus. "Now I go all over the world and tell others what God has done for me. If God can do it for me, He can do it for you." I heard those words, and I said to myself, "God can do that for me? You mean God really loves me and wants to have a relationship with me? That God would let his beloved son die in my place to call me His son."

I was overwhelmed with that peace again. He then offered an invitation: "If you would like to receive Jesus as your Savior and Lord, if you want a new start, and to let go of all your regrets and guilt, come down to this altar. God will save you now," he said, "Your life will never be the same again." I turned to my friend, who was a Christian, to explain what the man meant. My friend told me he was asking if you would like to invite Jesus into your life and be born again. "Is that something you want to do?" I said "Yes," this friend responded, "He spoke to me too. I'm a Christian, but I'm away from God so I suggested, 'I'll go if you go with me.'" So we then got out of our seats, walked down to the front of the church, and got on our knees. The evangelist began to lead us in prayer. As we prayed, I felt all my regrets and shame fall away, and my guilt was removed like heavily coated dirt washed off a window, allowing light in. After we finished praying, I knew something had happened to me. I felt as though I was brand new. Free from all the past, and it seemed as though I was literally born anew. That very moment, I became a new person in Christ. Second Corinthians 5:17 says that anyone who belongs to Christ has become a new person. The old life is gone. A new life has begun!

You may be thinking, "Wow, that's an amazing story. But that's not me." It's not by accident you're reading this right now. My friend, I want you to know that God had me write this booklet just for you. Just like He showed his love to me. He's revealing his love to you right now. He has gone to great lengths to get this information into your hands. He loves you so much. Remember, John 3:16 says, "For God so loved the world that he gave his only begotten son, that whosoever believes in him should not perish but have everlasting life." To perish means to be separated from God for eternity in a place called hell. Our sin is what sends us there. You see, we have all sinned and fallen short of the glory of God (Romans 3:23). There is a wage for sin. It's called death. Romans 6:23 says we were all going there. All of us have sinned against God. There was no one righteous, not one. That's why Jesus came to take away sin once and for all. He came to reconcile you and me back to God. You see, in the second part of Romans 6:23, it says, "But the gift of God is eternal life in Christ Jesus, our Lord."

Today, God wants to give you the free gift of eternal life. He wants to give you a brand-new life and make you part of his family. As his child, you can have peace, joy, freedom, healing, and prosperity. He loves you that much. You see, God didn't send Jesus into the world to condemn the world or to condemn you (John 3:17). No, a thousand times, no! You're condemned already. He sent Jesus to save you and give you abundant life (John 10:10). What you're feeling right now is God's love calling you. That conviction you are experiencing is God's way of drawing you to himself. He is knocking on the door of your heart. He says if you open the door, he will come in and dine with you and you with him (Revelations 3:20). Your life will never be the same.

Romans 10:13 says whoever calls on the name of the Lord shall be saved! Allow me to pray with you right now. Pray these words with me:

Dear Heavenly Father, I believe Jesus is the

Son of God. I believe he came into this world and died on a cross from me. He took all my sins so I could receive all his righteousness. I repent of my sins, and I ask you now to forgive me for all of them. Jesus, come into my heart. Make me a new creation. Save me now and be the Lord of my life. Thank you, Father, that I am saved, forgiven, and free. I am now a child of God! In Jesus's name, Amen.

Praise God, if you just prayed that prayer, you are now a new creation in Christ. Your new life has come, and your old life is gone (2 Corinthians 5:17). This is the beginning of the greatest adventure of your life.

God has great plans for you. Get you a good Bible to read and immerse yourself in the word daily, and he will speak to you. Ask the Father to fill you with His Holy Spirit (Luke 11:13). The Holy Spirit will give you wonderful prayer language (Acts 1:8, Acts 2:1–4, Acts 2:38, Acts 8:14, Acts 10:44–46, and Acts 19:1–7). Ask the Lord to send you to the local church He has for you so you can grow in Him with other believers.

Praise God, you can follow our ministry with all our links below. You will be encouraged in your walk with the Lord. God bless you, and welcome to the family!

Contact: Dan Miller Ministries
PO Box 1234
Cullman, AL 35056
(256) 636-7848
Email: danmillerministries@yahoo.com
Facebook: @danmillerministries
YouTube: Dan Miller Ministries

About the Author

Dan Miller is an ordained minister and a graduate of Rhema Bible College. Today, Dan is the founder of Dan Miller Ministries. A worldwide evangelism ministry that has answered the call to go into all the world and preach the gospel to every creature (Mk. 16:15). Dan's passion is to help others find the abundant life that Jesus died to give them (Jn. 10:10). Dan and his wife, Sherissa, have been married for twenty-three years. They have four children and reside in Cullman, Alabama.